The Ten Biggest Mistakes

That Can Wreck Your Washington Accident Case

The Essential Guide To Accident Cases in Washington State

The Ten Biggest Mistakes

That Can Wreck Your Washington Accident Case

Christopher M. Davis
Attorney at Law

Third Edition

Third Edition

Copyright © 2013 by Christopher Michael Davis

Printed in the United States of America.

ISBN: 978-1-59571-907-2

Designed and published by

Word Association Publishers
205 Fifth Avenue
Tarentum, Pennsylvania 15084

www.wordassociation.com
1.800.827.7903

Contents

Foreword

You may have been injured in an accident, or know someone who has. Either way, requesting this book was a good choice. If you're like me, you do your homework before making an important decision. And believe me, you do have an important decision to make. At some point you must decide how you want to pursue your accident case. Do you hire an attorney? Or do you go it alone? If you go it alone, then how do you deal with the insurance adjustor? What information is important? What potential traps lie ahead? This book can help. If you're thinking about hiring a lawyer then this book can help you on your search for an experienced and qualified accident attorney (commonly called a personal injury attorney). You'll find helpful tips on what to look for in a personal injury attorney, and how to "navigate" the numerous attorney ads that are placed in the yellow pages and on TV. This book also debunks some of the common myths associated with injury or accident claims and the attorneys that handle them. So read this book from front to back. It will probably be the best initial decision you make about your accident case. And if you should have further questions, you can contact me without obligation. My contact information is listed at the back of this book.

Christopher M. Davis

January 2007

Introduction

My wife and I host an annual party at our home each summer. At our party in the summer of 2006, I was approached by one of our guests. He told me he had been in a car accident a few months back and he wanted some advice on how to deal with the insurance company representing the other driver. As I gave him some general feedback, he asked more and more detailed questions about his case. What should he do with his own insurance company? (who by now was asking that he sign various forms and demanding that he attend a medical examination) Can he settle his own case without a lawyer? How? What was his case worth? The questions kept on coming. I was essentially "cornered" for almost an hour. Now, this wasn't the first time I had been asked these types of questions at a social gathering. In fact, it usually happened whenever my wife and I would meet new people at a party. As soon as someone discovered that I was a "personal injury lawyer" they would usually start out by saying to me, "You know, my brother (or wife, father, mother, etc.…) was injured in an accident, and now he's having trouble with the insurance company.…"

After our party I was telling my wife about being "cornered" by yet another person asking me for advice about his accident claim. She turned to me and said, "You know, you really ought to write a book." "A book about what?" I replied. "About accidents and insurance companies," she said. "That way people could simply read your book and you wouldn't have to answer the same questions you get over and over." Alas, she was right (as often was the case). And the idea for my book was born.

Chapter One

What is a Personal Injury or Accident Case?

When a lawyer says he or she handles "personal injury" or "accident" cases, just what does that mean? A personal injury case, accident case, or wrongful death case, is any type of claim where a person has been injured, disabled, maimed or killed due to the carelessness of another. The law has a special name for someone whose carelessness causes injury or death – it is called negligence. Certainly people can be negligent, but so can corporations and governmental entities. If someone's carelessness caused damage only to property (e.g., car, truck, equipment, home, etc.) but did not inflict injury on another person, then this is called a "property damage case" and not a personal injury case. Many personal injury attorneys, including this author, will not handle a property damage case unless the person also has suffered injuries.

Lawyers who have experience handling "personal injury" or "accident" cases will know how to gather the specific evidence needed to best support your claim, and prove your claim in court if necessary. This evidence may include witness testimony, medical and financial records, photographs, expert reports, exhibits and illustrations. Personal injury attorneys, if experienced, usually have strong negotiating skills and are adept at communicating with the insurance company claims representative. The lawyers who specialize in this area of the law are usually very familiar with the rules governing insurance contracts, claims handling, court procedure, the law of negligence, and proving damages.

A good personal injury lawyer should also have extensive knowledge in different fields of study. These may include accident reconstruction, medicine, vocational rehabilitation, biomechanics, economics and engineering. Often times the information in one or more of these fields is necessary to prove the case in court or it may simply help the lawyer achieve a good result in your case. And finally, a personal injury lawyer should be very experienced with arguing and presenting cases in court, especially in front of a jury.

Lawyers who try personal injury cases in court, particularly in front of juries, must have above average trial skills, extensive experience and hard-earned intuition. The good personal injury attorney must also have excellent persuasion and oratory skills when presenting the case in court so that jurors will be motivated to decide the case in favor of the attorney's client. It is also important that the personal injury lawyer have extensive experience in trying accident cases.

Because of the nuances involved with personal injury law, it is not sufficient that the lawyer usually tries other types of cases (like criminal defense or divorce trials). A lawyer who has experience trying personal injury cases in front of juries and getting good results can usually command the highest settlement offer from the insurance company when compared with a lawyer who has never or rarely tried such a case.

Chapter Two

You Entered Into a War Zone As Soon As You Were Injured

Did you know that the day you were injured you entered a war zone with the insurance industry? Over the past 30+ years, the insurance industry has spent billions of dollars on advertising to spread false and misleading information about accident claims. The industry wants people to believe that the justice system is out of control and that people who file lawsuits are getting millions of dollars for minor injuries. Such propaganda has created the false perception among the public that the system needs fixing. Unfortunately, this "misinformation" spread by the insurance industry has had an enormous negative influence on juries and their verdicts. Juries today are highly skeptical of people who file lawsuits that claim money for "pain and suffering." Many people who wind up on juries believe the myths touted by the insurance industry. This can be a huge obstacle to achieving justice in your case, even when the injuries are severe and negligence has been established. Lawyers who handle these cases have learned over the past few years that it is much more difficult to achieve justice for their clients. You need to be aware that the insurance claims adjustor will utilize any means necessary to pay out as little as possible, even on legitimate claims that involve serious injuries. Insurance adjustors receive extensive training on how to save the company money, and not necessarily on how to examine a claim and pay a fair settlement. Many insurance companies reward their adjustors with bonuses or promotions based on how much money that person saves the company rather than how many claims are settled. The claims adjustor accomplishes this in several ways:

* ***Using Delay.*** The adjustor is a master of using delay tactics to wear people down. He knows that many people will at some point throw up their hands and say "Enough!" while finally accepting the company's last offer just to be done with the whole process.
* ***Requesting Unnecessary Information.*** Another method is when the adjustor makes repeated requests for "documentation" even if the information will have little or no bearing on the amount that will be offered in settlement. Repeated requests for unnecessary documentation can easily frustrate people and wear them down so they're more likely to accept a lower settlement offer.

* ***Disputing the Medical Treatment.*** One way the adjustor will minimize your claim is to dispute or question your need for medical treatment, despite having no medical training! (even if the treatment is prescribed by your own doctor!). Many times it does not matter to the adjustor that your treatment has been recommended by a reputable licensed physician.

* ***"Nickel & Dime" the Medical Charges.*** Often times the adjustor will only agree to "accept" 70, 80 or 90% of your past medical charges, while having no medical background to support such a position. By "nickel and diming" the consumer, the well-trained adjustor knows that most people will not hire a lawyer to challenge a small portion of the medical bills.

* ***Tell You Not to Hire an Attorney.*** Other times the insurance company will dissuade you from hiring an experienced attorney and falsely tell you that any money you receive will go only to the attorney. Still other times the adjustor may threaten to "deny" or "lowball" the claim if you hire a lawyer.

* ***Misrepresenting Insurance Policy Benefits.*** Sometimes the adjustor will misrepresent the amount of insurance coverage that is available to you. Or worse, the adjustor doesn't even tell you that the insurance coverage or certain types of benefits even exist. This tactic may also be used to entice you

into accepting a smaller settlement than what would otherwise be warranted.

* ***Acting as Your Friend.*** There are times when the claims adjustor will "befriend" you and make it appear that she is watching out for your interests when in fact she is not. Sometimes the adjustor will give you advice about the type or frequency of your medical treatment, and then decide later on not to pay for the treatment because it is "excessive."

* ***Making False Promises.*** There are times when the adjustor will make promises to you that he or she knows can't be met. For example, this author had a client who was promised that the insurance company would continue to pay her medical bills every month until she recovered. This went on for four months until the adjustor decided that four months of treatment was enough. The problem was that the client didn't find out about the insurance company's decision to stop paying until she had racked up many more months of medical bills!

These are just a few of the tactics that the insurance industry uses to badger and wear down injured victims so that less money is paid out. And to a large extent, the industry has been successful. The strong backlash created by the insurance industry against our justice system is a very strong movement in many parts of our country.

The movement has a name, it is called Tort Reform. The success of the Tort Reform movement has emboldened the insurance industry to withhold fair settlements until you convince them that you are ready, willing and able to go to trial. But do not be discouraged. You CAN achieve fair compensation for your injuries and beat the insurance industry at their own game. But it may take time and effort.

Case Study:

Insurance Company Nailed for Engaging In Illegal Claims Practices

Some insurance companies use fraudulent tactics to trick accident victims into accepting very small settlements. Take Allstate Insurance Company for example. This carrier had a policy of deceiving accident victims into believing that the company was representing their interests in settling the claim.

In 1997 Janet Jones was severely injured when a teenager ran a stop sign and t-boned her vehicle. The impact of the crash hurled Jones's minivan onto its side. A defective seatbelt caused her to be partially ejected from the van. She sustained severe head and facial injuries, including the loss of an eye. The medical expenses from her initial hospital stay grew to more than $75,000—exceeding the $25,000 liability limit on the teenager's Allstate policy.

Three days after the accident, Allstate claims adjusters contacted Jones with a form letter promoting its "Quality Service Pledge." Allstate said it would serve as Jones's claims representative for the accident. Allstate's claims adjusters continued to contact Jones and asked the Jones family to "trust" Allstate and reaffirmed the company's commitment to make an "appropriate offer of compensation" for her injuries. However, Allstate adjusters cautioned the Jones family that Allstate would not continue to represent them in the claims process if they retained an attorney. Allstate then falsely told Mrs. Jones that she needed to settle with the company for the amount of the teenager's policy limits. But by doing so, Mrs. Jones would have relinquished her claim against the manufacturer that made the defective seat belt, causing her to lose virtually hundreds of thousands of dollars in settlement proceeds. By settling with Allstate, Mrs. Jone's settlement only benefited the insurance company.

After Mrs. Jones filed suit against Allstate, her attorney obtained the company's training manuals. These materials showed that Allstate's adjusters were instructed to bilk injured citizens. They were trained to contact accident victims immediately after the accident and then portray themselves as representatives for the claims process. Allstate also had a policy of routinely sending accident victims a letter promising a "Quality Service Pledge" with a brochure telling accident victims that they "do not need attorneys to receive fair treatment or a fair settlement." Allstate's explicit goal was to remove attorneys from the claims process entirely so it could pay out less money to claimants and thereby increase its own revenue.

The Washington State Supreme Court ruled that Allstate engaged in the illegal practice of law by advising Mrs. Jones to accept a settlement that only benefited the company.[1] Fortunately, Mrs. Jones was allowed to recover damages against this insurance company. There have been more than 50 similar lawsuits filed against Allstate for its claims practices nationwide.

Chapter Three

Do You Really Need an Attorney for Your Accident Case?

You definitely do not need an attorney for every small accident case. What is a small accident case? There are no hard and fast rules, but usually a small case involves an accident with no damage, or little damage, to the vehicle and where the treatment and/or injuries last no more than a few months. In a small case, the medical bills usually don't exceed a few thousand dollars. And the injuries are not usually considered permanent. These are cases that can often be settled or resolved without the assistance of an attorney. In my practice, I tell clients that it may not be cost effective to use an attorney for a small case because most of the recovery may go to pay the attorney and you may be left with very little afterwards. In small cases, I tell the person that he or she may have just as good a chance at recovering a settlement near or equal to one that the attorney can get for you. With a small case, the person may be better served by handling the case on his or her own and without the assistance of an attorney. But if you feel comfortable gathering evidence and records to support your claim and negotiating with the insurance adjustor, then you may not need the assistance of an attorney. However, the bigger the case the more likely you will benefit from using an experienced attorney. That is, in a bigger case you will likely recover more compensation for your injuries with the assistance of a lawyer than without (even after subtracting the lawyer's fee). Why is this so? Because the attorney has specialized knowledge and the legal authority to go to court, thereby forcing the insurance company to incur more expense by having to hire its own attorney(s). The experienced personal injury attorney usually has a better understanding of what the claim is worth and then can often effectively communicate the value of the claim to the insurance adjustor. Unless you're in the business of settling and litigating injury cases, the person without an attorney may be at a serious disadvantage when dealing with a seasoned insurance claims representative.

Before you decide on whether to hire an attorney...

Did you know that a 1999 study found that insurance companies pay higher settlements to injured people who use an attorney than those who do not?

Yes, it's true. In 1999 the insurance industry performed a study to find out if people who had accident claims received more money in settlement by using an attorney than those people who settled on their own. The study was performed by the Insurance Research Council, a non-profit organization that is supported by leading property and casualty insurance companies across the United States. The mission of the IRC is to advance the insurance industry's view on matters crucial to insurance companies.[2] The IRC found that people who used an attorney received on average 3½ times more money in settlement than those individuals who settled on their own. Often times accident victims are told by the insurance adjustor that they shouldn't hire a lawyer because they will receive less money in settlement. This study shows that this simply is not true.

Chapter Four
How Do You Determine the Value of a Personal Injury Case?

There is no magic formula or process by which someone can predict with certainty the amount of money that a personal injury case may be worth. If there were, then society wouldn't have a need for personal injury lawyers. One could simply apply the "formula" to come up with the value of a case. And if this happened there would be no need for a trial. Yet we know that trials are necessary when the two sides cannot agree on the value of a case.

Generally speaking, a case is worth the amount of damages inflicted on the person who has been injured. These damages may be easy to calculate, like past and future medical charges, lost earnings, lost earning capacity, and property loss. But the law also states that the injured person has the right to recover compensation for other "intangible" harms. It is these "intangible" harms that are more difficult to calculate, and they usually include pain, agony, disability, loss of enjoyment, inconvenience, and mental anguish. The intangible harms are purely subjective, difficult to determine and often vary among the people (or jurors) who are deciding the case. Ultimately, the value of a case is determined by the jury (or judge if the case is tried to the court).

After a case arises, the injured person's attorney and the at-fault person's insurance company (and the defense attorney if the case is in litigation) are continually trying to evaluate how a jury might see the case and how much money a jury might award. Then each side will assign a value or a value range, and try to negotiate a settlement close or above each side's own range.

Often times it may take many months or years before the value of a case can be adequately assessed. One reason for this is because of the slow progress of the person's recovery or rehabilitation. Another reason is due to the complexity of the injury or condition which may cause a significant delay in a firm diagnosis by the treating physician. In many instances a case should not be settled or resolved until the person obtains maximum improvement following the accident, and this can also contribute to the delay of achieving a reasonable resolution of the case.

In many instances the value of a case is driven primarily by the extent and severity of the person's injuries. Other important factors to consider include the type, extent and frequency of past medical treatment and the need for future treatment. When I evaluate a case, I also rely on several other factors to help me determine the case value. These factors may include, but are not limited to, the client's likeability[3] as a witness and his or her credibility, the facts of the accident giving rise to the case, the extent and permanency of the injuries, the client's age, whether the client missed time from work, the identities of the at-fault insurance company and its defense attorney, specific legal or evidentiary issues involved in the case, the county or venue where the case has been or will be filed, and the amount of settlements and verdicts for similar types of cases that I and other lawyers have handled in the past.

You should note that no two cases are alike, even if the accident and/or injuries involved are nearly identical. This means that the evaluation of two cases which appear to be similar on the surface may actually produce widely different evaluations due to the other factors listed above. Evaluating personal injury cases takes a lot of knowledge, experience and some hard-earned intuition. Without these traits you may be at a serious disadvantage when negotiating with the insurance adjustor. And unless you are in the business of evaluating and settling personal injury cases for a living, you should look to an experienced personal injury attorney for guidance.

Chapter Five

The Legal Process for Personal Injury Cases

Often times trying to negotiate a reasonable settlement with the insurance company is a waste of time. More and more insurance companies are taking a very aggressive stance in settling accident claims. Certain carriers have a reputation for making unreasonably low settlement offers, even if the injuries are severe. Often times the insurance companies use pre-lawsuit negotiations to find out as much as possible about you, your lawyer and your doctors. This can result in the unfair advantage to the insurance company not to mention a complete waste of time and effort for you. For these reasons, it may be advantageous to file a lawsuit immediately and then continue negotiating the claim if possible. Once a lawsuit is filed, the court will set certain deadlines including a trial date. These deadlines, and in particular a trial date, can help motivate the insurance company to make reasonable and diligent attempts to settle the case.

To start a lawsuit, papers must be filed in court and a filing fee paid. These papers are called a "summons" and "complaint." When a person files a lawsuit he or she is called the "plaintiff." The person or corporation that is being sued is called the "defendant." The plaintiff must personally serve a copy of the summons and complaint on the defendant. You only have a certain amount of time to settle your case or file a lawsuit and then personally serve the defendant. In Washington, this time is usually three years from the date of the accident.[4] This deadline is called the "statute of limitations." It is a dangerous practice to wait to settle your claim right before the statute of limitations period expires. If you have to file suit right before the deadline and you cannot find the defendant or if you serve the wrong defendant, your case could be dismissed and you get nothing. For this reason, you should not wait to hire an attorney right before the statute of limitations is about to expire. Many attorneys, including myself, refuse to accept a case where there may be insufficient time to investigate the case, file suit and locate and personally serve the defendant.

After the lawsuit is filed and the defendant is served, both sides participate in a process of asking for and exchanging information about the case. This process is called "discovery." Each side is allowed to investigate what evidence and witnesses may be used at trial. The discovery process may entail sending or answering written questions (called interrogatories) and requests for documents and other tangible materials that are relevant to the case. The defendant's attorney will also be allowed to access your medical records and work history, including your financial records.

The discovery process may also include depositions. A deposition is a face-to-face meeting where the attorneys are allowed to ask a witness questions under oath while a court reporter transcribes the session. Any witness that may offer testimony at trial can be deposed, including you, your doctors, and your friends and family. If your deposition is requested, it is very important that you prepare for this with your attorney. Your conduct at the deposition can influence the value assigned to the case and also affect the likelihood of whether the case will settle before trial.

When a lawsuit involves a claim for personal injuries, the other side may be permitted to have their own doctor examine you. Therefore, the discovery phase may also include a request by the other side that you submit to a medical examination and/or psychological evaluation. There are specific criteria to be satisfied before an involuntary medical examination of the plaintiff is allowed. In my office, we have a fairly specific stipulation that must be signed by the other side which imposes several conditions and restrictions on how the examination may proceed.

Depending on which county your lawsuit is filed in and the complexity of the case, the discovery phase can take many months or sometimes years. When discovery is completed, and each side knows what evidence will be offered at trial, this is the time when the parties may conduct settlement discussions. Sometimes the parties will engage in alternative ways to resolve the case, like mediation. In mediation, the parties agree to hire a retired judge or an experienced attorney who will assist the parties in reaching a settlement. Mediation is voluntary and nonbinding (unless a settlement is reached). A mediation session is also confidential so anything that is said during the session cannot be used at trial. Many times mediation can be used to successfully resolve a case. Mediation sessions can occur in one day or last several days depending on the size and/or complexity of the case.

If you fail to settle the case after discovery has ended, the case will then proceed to trial. Each side has the option of trying the case before a judge or jury. If a jury is requested by one side, a jury demand must be filed in court and a fee must be paid. The court rules usually require that certain documents must be filed and exchanged within 30 to 60 days before the trial date. These documents may include witness and exhibit lists, motions, trial memorandums, and jury instructions.

Mandatory Arbitration – the alternative to trial.

In Washington, most of the superior courts have adopted a program known as "mandatory arbitration." Arbitration is another way to resolve a case instead of going to trial. With arbitration, the court appoints an "arbitrator" who will decide the case by listening to testimony, reviewing evidence, and then issuing an award. The arbitrator is usually an experienced attorney or retired judge. This author has served as an arbitrator in many personal injury cases.

The purpose of Mandatory Arbitration is to reduce court congestion, expedite the litigation process, and to provide a cost effective resolution of civil claims. Arbitration is often preferred over a jury trial because the costs are much lower, the rules of evidence are relaxed, and the hearing itself is far less stressful than a jury trial. Also, the arbitration hearing may be scheduled within four to six months after a lawsuit is filed while it can take up to two years or more to get to trial. Most arbitration hearings last no longer than a day while a jury trial can last several days or even weeks.

There are potential drawbacks with arbitration. For instance, there is a limit on the amount of damages that can be awarded. In Washington (as of the date of this writing) that limit is now $50,000. But even if your case is worth more than $50,000 it could still be advantageous to participate in mandatory arbitration because of the high costs and risks of going to trial. Another potential drawback is that either party can appeal the arbitration award and request that the case be tried in court. However, if a party appeals the award but fails to do better at trial, that party will have to pay the other side's attorney fees and costs (which could be substantial depending on the facts of the case and the length of trial).

In this author's experience, more than 90% of the arbitration appeals are requested by the defendant's insurance company. Most plaintiff attorneys do not like to appeal an arbitration award because it creates a significant risk that the client may have to pay the defendant's attorney's fees. What most people fail to recognize is that many insurance companies will intentionally appeal a fair arbitration award to force the plaintiff to incur the substantial added expense of trying the case in court. Why is this so? Because these same insurance companies want to make it as expensive and time consuming as possible to wear down the plaintiff and her attorney. In fact, many insurance companies will routinely spend more money to defend a case than the amount of money it would take to simply pay the arbitration award.

If the arbitration award is appealed and the case goes to trial, the jury will never be informed that the case was submitted to arbitration. And of course, the jury will never be told the amount of the arbitrator's award. This can create problems especially in smaller cases because the jury may be left with the impression that the plaintiff and his or her attorney have forced the jury to come to court to decide a small case. Many times jurors resent having to decide a small case because they believe smaller cases should be settled. Yet jurors never realize until after the trial that it was the defendant's insurance company that appealed the award and forced a trial. Fortunately, this author has developed proven trial techniques to combat this problem.

It is important to remember that there are specific rules that govern Mandatory Arbitration. These rules are complex and can provide traps to the inexperienced attorney. You should always consult with a qualified and experienced personal injury attorney about whether your accident case is appropriate for Mandatory Arbitration.

Chapter Six
How to Choose the Right Attorney for your Accident Case

If you've ever browsed through the "yellow pages" of your local phone book, you'll often find numerous advertisements (some times dozens of pages) for personal injury attorneys. These ads usually say the same things: "Free Consultation" "No Recovery, No Fee" "We'll Protect Your Rights!," "Aggressive Representation!" or "Need a Lawyer?" How on earth does someone who has never had to hire an attorney wade through all of these ads and find a qualified personal injury attorney, let alone someone that is good??

Finding a good personal injury attorney can be challenging, but not impossible. Here are some guidelines, which if followed, should make your search easier and also relieve some anxiety.

* ✳ *Choose an attorney who specializes in personal injury.* There are many attorneys who represent personal injury clients in addition to other practice areas, such as divorce, criminal defense or real

estate. You should pick an attorney whose practice is devoted 100% to personal injury law. The field of personal injury is too complicated for a "generalist" or "part-time" lawyer to master. If you needed surgery on your shoulder, would you rather see a "general" surgeon who performs surgery on many different areas of the body, or a surgeon who only does "shoulder surgery?" Most people would choose the specialist. Don't take chances with your personal injury claim by hiring a "generalist."

✳ ***Choose an attorney who demonstrates expertise in the field of personal injury law.*** There are too many different types of the law for any one attorney to claim specialty in multiple areas. No one can do everything well. Most people want to see a specialist. The same is true for lawyers. The field of personal injury law is complex with subtle nuances that could mean the difference between recovering a few hundred dollars versus several thousands of dollars. The attorney you choose should limit his or her practice exclusively to personal injury law. Does the attorney write about personal injury? Has the lawyer lectured or taught other lawyers about personal injury law? If yes, these are good signs that the lawyer is a personal injury specialist.

✳ ***Choose an attorney who understands the medicine involved in your case.*** This is a no-brainer, right?

But you would be very surprised at how many attorneys who claim specialty in personal injury have little understanding of the medicine and treatment involved with the client's injury. For example, take a case involving neck and back injuries. These types of injuries can be difficult to prove in court because spine medicine is extremely complex and the diagnostic imaging may show very little or nothing at all. Yet, this area of medicine has also undergone enormous strides and advances just in the last ten years. There are now new diagnoses in the area of spine medicine that literally did not exist a few years ago, not to mention new treatments and minimally invasive procedures that have been created due to advancements in technology. If you have a neck or back injury claim, you obviously want an attorney who understands spine medicine so proper treatment and diagnoses can easily be pursued or presented to the insurance company in negotiations, or made part of a persuasive presentation to a jury on your behalf. You would be surprised at how few personal injury attorneys really understand this area of medicine yet neck and back injury claims make up the bulk of accident cases that exist in Washington.

✳ ***Choose an attorney who actually goes to trial.*** I know, I know. If you're like most people who have a claim for injuries, you'd rather not have to go to trial. So why pick an attorney who actually does regularly try injury cases? To understand why this is such an extremely important factor when choosing an attorney you have to understand the business of insurance and why claims are settled. Essentially, the insurance company is in the business of "risk." That is, it accepts your money with the promise that it will pay you money if you encounter certain risks of harm or damage. The risks are usually low, which is why the insurance company can earn enormous profits. When it comes to paying a claim, the company only pays a "settlement" if there is a "risk" that the company may have to pay more if the person files a lawsuit and goes to trial. Attorneys who regularly go to trial increase the insurance company's "risk" that it might have to pay much more money if the jury awards more than the last settlement offer. Insurance companies regularly keep lists of the personal injury attorneys who do go to trial. These are the attorneys who can command premium settlement offers compared to attorneys who do not go to trial. Simply put, the insurance company will pay more money to settle a case if there's a greater chance that the attorney will try the case in court. That is why having an attorney who has a reputation of going to trial can actually increase your chances of avoiding trial.

* *Choose an attorney who wins at trial.* This goes without saying. An attorney who gets results at trial is the insurance company's worst nightmare. The carrier will pay much more money to settle a case if the injured person's attorney has a track record of winning at trial than if the attorney does not. Choose an attorney that knows how to win.

* *Beware of attorneys who actively solicit you.* You should be cautious of attorneys who contact you in writing just after you or a loved one has been injured, maimed or killed in an accident. Most state bar associations have rules against attorney solicitation, or at least have very stringent limitations on this sort of activity. I have no respect for attorneys who feel the need to cross the line by actively soliciting clients right after the accident. If an attorney engages in this sort of unethical behavior it may give some indication how that attorney might perform in your case.

* *Be cautious of attorneys who advertise on T.V. or take out big flashy ads in yellow pages or other publications.* Did you know that many of the T.V. and yellow page ads for lawyers are paid for by attorneys who have never actually tried a personal injury case in court? In fact, some of these advertisements are created by law firms that have a "policy" of always settling their cases without ever filing a lawsuit! If you were an insurance adjustor who knew that a

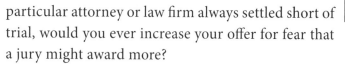

particular attorney or law firm always settled short of trial, would you ever increase your offer for fear that a jury might award more?

✳ ***Understand bar association referral lists.*** Many local bar associations operate a "referral list" where consumers can get the name of an attorney. Just understand that the lawyer has signed up and paid a fee to be included on the referral list. Some but not all of these referral lists don't bother to check or verify the attorney's experience with the type of case that is being referred.

✳ ***The likeable lawyer is not enough.*** There are many people who choose to hire an attorney based solely on whether the attorney is likeable. I know of some very personable and likeable lawyers who claim to do personal injury law, but whom I would never recommend based on their limited experience and expertise. Would you let a likeable surgeon operate on your body if you knew the doctor rarely made it to the operating room? It is important that you like your attorney, or at least respect him or her, but it should not provide the only basis for your hiring decision.

✳ ***Choose an attorney who you feel comfortable with.*** You should feel comfortable with the lawyer and his or her ability to communicate with you. Does the attorney seem credible and trustworthy? Does the attorney explain everything to your satisfaction, or does he explain why an answer to a particular question can't be given at that time? You should feel comfortable with the lawyer. You should also understand how the two of you will be working together on your case.

Case Study:
T.V. Lawyer Nailed for False Advertising

Don't believe everything you see on T.V. Arizona lawyer Stephen M. Zang and his partner ran numerous T.V. commercials and other massive print advertising to market their young 4 year-old law firm. The campaign was hugely successful – it managed to produce over 1600 personal injury cases in just four years. The ads contained the following statements:

* We are a personal injury law firm with the medical experience to understand complicated injuries.
* We have investigators to find witnesses and hidden evidence.
* We perform detailed preparation in your case, and the better your case is prepared for trial, the more likely your case will settle out of court.
* If you are in an accident, you need more than a lawyer's words.

The ads included dramatic footage or scenes showing accidents, books about accidents and medicine, a judge in a courtroom, and a picture showing the attorney arguing before a jury in the courtroom.

Upon investigation, the Supreme Court of Arizona discovered the following:

* No attorney at the firm had ever tried a personal injury case in court or to its conclusion.
* Mr. Zang, who was pictured in ads arguing a case in front of a jury, admitted that he was not competent to try personal injury cases.
* The firm had an express policy of not taking cases to trial.
* In those cases where trial was necessary, the policy was to refer the case to a competent personal injury attorney who would try the case in court for a cut of the fee.
* Although the firm's policy was to settle all cases, the clients were not told this.
* Clients were never informed about the attorneys' lack of experience or that their case would be referred to another attorney if trial was necessary.

Mr. Zang and his law partner were found to have committed numerous ethics violations. They were disbarred by the Arizona Supreme Court.

Chapter Seven
What You Need to Know About Lawyer Advertising

You need to know a few things about lawyer advertising. For example, if you look through the yellow pages you'll see that the ads placed by attorneys all say essentially the same thing. Very few of them actually give good useful information to make it easier for you to choose a good lawyer for your case. Although the yellow pages are a good place to get names of attorneys, you need to be aware of the following points when it comes to lawyer advertising:

* There is no rule which requires that the lawyer have a minimum amount of experience handling the case which the lawyer wants to advertise.
* Although the bar association has rules that govern lawyer advertising, it usually does not actively investigate, restrict or determine whether each lawyer who advertises is a specialist or has experience with the type of case being advertised. This means a lawyer can advertise that she is a "divorce lawyer"

or "personal injury attorney" when that lawyer may have limited experience or knowledge of that area of the law.

* There are virtually no restrictions on the different types of law that the lawyer wants to advertise. Therefore, you should be extremely careful about choosing an attorney based solely on that attorney's advertising claim, whether the ad is in the phone book or on television.

* Any attorney can buy a big slick ad in the yellow pages. The phone book company typically does not verify the claims that are being made in the ad. In many cases the phone book company does not even verify that the person is a licensed attorney in good standing! Use caution.

* A lawyer who advertises does not mean that that lawyer will be handling your case. Some lawyers simply run advertisements and then refer out most or all of the clients to other lawyers to do the work in exchange for a referral fee. Such a lawyer essentially acts like a referral broker. Be especially cautious of ads placed by out of state attorneys. Because of state licensing requirements, these attorneys will usually have to refer the case to a lawyer who is licensed to practice law in Washington.

* A lawyer who purchases full page ads in the yellow pages, or pays for slick T.V. commercials, does not

necessarily mean that the lawyer is super successful. Some lawyers who pay for such advertising operate a "volume practice" for the purpose of making just a little money on the numerous cases that are generated from the ad. Many times a "volume practice" attorney tries to settle all or most of the cases to earn the most amount of money in the least amount of time. The only time you may see this lawyer is if his face appears in the ad!

* Some lawyers who run big ads to fill their "volume practices" will rarely even work on a case. These lawyers farm out every aspect of the case to a paralegal or legal assistant. The only time the lawyer may even look at your case is after it has settled and the lawyer wants to collect his fee!

* Be cautious of lawyer ads that create unjustified expectations. For example, if the lawyer advertises that he can obtain "Fast Settlements in 30 Days" he probably never goes to trial and settles cases for far less than what they are actually worth. In most cases, good settlements take time and effort.

* Sometimes the lawyer's advertising can negatively affect your own case. If your case goes to trial and jurors recognize your lawyer from his advertising, it may undermine your lawyer's credibility during trial. Do you want jurors to remember your lawyer as the one who can get "BIG MONEY DAMAGES!!" or

"FAST SETTLEMENTS $$$" for pain and suffering?? Jurors watch television, too, you know.

Lawyer TV Ads: A word to the wise

Did you know that there are companies that offer prewritten and pre-shot TV commercials for personal injury attorneys? You've probably seen one. Sometimes a famous actor is used (like Robert Vaughan, William Shatner or Eric Estrada). Other times an attractive man or woman is shown speaking behind a desk or holding a legal book or doing something else to act like a lawyer. The person says something like, "If you've been in an accident, get the money you deserve. Speak to an attorney for free. Call 1-800-XXXXXXX." What you need to know is that many times your call is routed to a call center that randomly sends your call to the next attorney "in line." The next one "in line" is an attorney who has actually paid a hefty fee to be on the "list." Any attorney with enough money can pay to be on the list, including attorneys who have never tried a case in court. Many times the attorney who has paid the fee is not necessarily the most experienced lawyer for your case. Now I'm not saying that all attorneys who use TV advertising are inexperienced. But you should not rely on TV advertising alone when choosing a lawyer. Just a word to the wise.

Case Study:

T.V. Personal Injury Lawyer Fails Client

Here's a sad story about a lawyer who advertised on T.V. in Rochester, New York. The attorney, Jim Schapiro, ran aggressive T.V. commercials which promised to obtain large financial settlements for victims, referred to himself as "the meanest, nastiest S.O.B. in town," and claimed to have aggressive courtroom prowess. Schapiro, who called himself "The Hammer," had law offices in the states of New York and Florida.

In 2002, one of Schapiro's clients, Christopher Wagner, sued Schapiro for malpractice. Mr. Wagner had been injured in a car accident and had responded to one of Mr. Schapiro's television ads. Mr. Wagner alleged that he had incurred medical bills of $182,000 but that Schapiro's firm advised him to accept a settlement of only $65,000 from the driver and then promised that he could get more money by filing suit against the state of New York. It turned out that the state had no liability for the accident and Schapiro never pursued Mr. Wagner's case further.

In a video deposition, Jim Schapiro testified that he had never tried a personal injury case in court and that he had been living in Florida for the last seven years. Mr. Wagner's attorney also discovered that Schapiro's Rochester law firm staffed just one lawyer who had only tried four cases. A New York jury found that Schapiro had engaged in misleading and deceptive advertising and that he committed malpractice. Schapiro was ordered to pay $1.5 million to Wagner.

Consequently, in 2004 Schapiro was suspended for practicing law for one year by the State of New York. In 2005, Schapiro was then suspended from practicing law in Florida for one year. In 2004, four additional clients sued Schapiro alleging that he had engaged in misleading advertising and had committed malpractice. Thereafter Schapiro stopped practicing law and instead now writes books for injury victims.

Chapter Eight

What A Personal Injury Lawyer Can Do For You

I can't speak for every personal injury attorney, but I can tell you what I do for my own clients in any given case:

* Initial interview with client
* Educate and teach clients about personal injury claims
* Educate and teach clients about the litigation process
* Gather written records and documents to support the claim, including medical records, police report, and employment records
* Perform investigation of the client's claim, including gathering witness statements, photographs, diagrams, and physical evidence
* Read and analyze the client's own automobile insurance policy to see what coverage is available to pay for the client's damages, like medical, hospital and wage loss benefits
* Meet and confer with the client's own medical doctors and other healthcare providers to fully understand client's condition

* Obtain specific reports from experts to support the client's claim
* Analyze any pertinent legal issues that may affect client's case, like contributory negligence, assumption of risk, comparative fault, etc.
* File necessary claim forms with the at-fault governmental agency
* Analyze client's own health insurance or governmental benefit plan to ascertain whether any money they spent must be repaid
* Analyze and address any liens asserted against the client's settlement recovery (various healthcare providers, insurers, governmental agencies may file liens seeking to be repaid money for benefits already paid to or on behalf of the client)
* Contact the insurance company about the claim and conduct periodic discussions with the carrier about your case so that appropriate reserves are set aside to settle the case
* Conduct negotiations with the insurance adjustor in an effort to settle the claim, either short of litigation or short of trial
* If a lawsuit will be filed, then prepare and draft the summons and complaint to file in court
* Perform investigation to locate the defendant so that personal service of the summons and complaint can be achieved

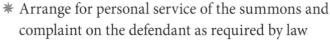

* Arrange for personal service of the summons and complaint on the defendant as required by law
* Prepare and draft written questions for information from the other side (called interrogatories and requests for production)
* Prepare the client for his or her deposition
* Prepare for and conduct the deposition of the defendant and other lay witnesses
* Meet with client's physicians to prepare for their own deposition requested by the defense attorney
* Prepare to take the deposition of the defendant's experts, including medical experts
* Prepare the client for his or her medical examination by the defendant's medical experts
* Answer questions and produce information and records requested by the other side
* Review and analyze the client's medical records and billings
* Hire other necessary experts to support or prove the client's claim, including other physicians, economists, engineers, vocational experts, etc.
* Review and analyze expert reports about the client's case
* File the necessary documents in court as required by the judge, including witness lists, trial readiness, settlement conferences, etc.
* Prepare the client and other witnesses for trial
* Create and prepare exhibits for trial

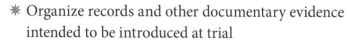

* Organize records and other documentary evidence intended to be introduced at trial
* Prepare for mediation and/or arbitration by organizing records and other documents for submission to the mediator or arbitrator
* Research and write briefs and file motions to keep out or let in certain evidence at trial
* Perform or participate in mock trials or focus groups to prepare for trial
* Try the case over the course of several days before a judge or jury
* Analyze verdict and research any issues that occurred at trial
* Write briefs or motions following verdict to obtain post-trial relief, including motions for attorney fees, or to overturn the verdict
* Analyze trial record to determine if appeal is warranted
* Research and write briefs and motions if appeal is filed
* Negotiate subrogation claims asserted by client's insurance company or governmental agency that provided benefits to client

Chapter Nine

The Ten Biggest Mistakes That Can Wreck Your Washington Accident Case

Over the years I have compiled a list of the Ten Biggest Mistakes that can Wreck Your Washington Accident Case. These mistakes are based on my extensive experience handling accident claims, as well as my discussions with judges and jurors following my trials. The ten biggest mistakes are as follows:

1. The client waits several days or weeks to receive medical care. If you are really hurt in an accident, it is extremely important that you promptly see the doctor. Sometimes people will delay treatment following an accident, thinking that their condition or pain will gradually improve or subside. When it doesn't, and you see the doctor for the first time several days or weeks after the accident, it can be extremely difficult to prove that your injury was caused by the accident and not something else.

This is a time where being "stoic" can actually hurt you if your injury turns out to be more severe. The more time that elapses following the accident before you first seek treatment the more difficult it may be to prove that either your injury was caused by the accident or that your injury is severe enough to justify a claim for compensation. Jurors expect an injured person to see a doctor promptly after the accident, particularly if you will be claiming compensation for that injury.

2. The client is referred to a doctor by a lawyer immediately after the accident. Jurors are highly suspicious of people who are referred to a doctor by a lawyer immediately after the accident, particularly if this is the first and only doctor that was seen. Similarly, jurors are suspicious of lawyers and doctors who have "referral" relationships that span many years. If a doctor has treated many of the lawyer's clients in the past year, that doctor's credibility with jurors becomes highly suspect. Many times jurors will reject the doctor's testimony if they believe the doctor has too close of a relationship with the lawyer. There are exceptions of course. For example, if your lawyer sends you to a doctor for a "second opinion" or if the lawyer suggests a group of specialists or doctors to address your injury long after the accident has occurred than this is usually not a problem. It is perfectly acceptable for your lawyer to hire a medical expert to examine you for the purpose of assisting the lawyer's evaluation of the case or to testify in court as an expert. There are no hard and fast rules here, so each case will depend on its own facts.

3. The client fails to obtain sufficient information at the accident scene and does not call the police. If you fail to obtain accurate information about the other driver, e.g., current address, driver license number, insurance information, etc., then this can cause substantial problems. How is the lawyer supposed to find and locate the at-fault driver to file a lawsuit if you did not obtain accurate information at the scene? Not calling the police can also be a big problem, especially if there is a dispute about who caused the accident. The police officer will often take down pertinent information, obtain statements from witnesses, and then file a report with the appropriate department. The report can then be obtained at a later date and used by your lawyer. If you have a camera, then taking photos of the vehicles and the accident scene might also help.

4. The client gives too much information to the at-fault driver's insurance company right after the accident. Often times the other insurance company asks you to give a "recorded statement" and sign medical authorizations which allow it to request current and prior medical records.

This is a big mistake. You can make what appears at first to be innocent statements, which then can be used later on to minimize your injuries or undermine your case. Giving the insurance company a medical release so it can go fishing into your past medical history can also give it ammunition to deny your claim or minimize your injuries. I wouldn't do it.

5. The client refuses to hire a lawyer, or delays hiring a lawyer, when the injuries may appear serious. If the claim is big enough to warrant the involvement of a personal injury attorney, then it is usually preferable to hire an attorney early in the claim. Often times the personal injury attorney can spot potential problems or anticipate defenses from the insurance company very early on in the claim process and take efforts to avoid them or minimize their impact. But if a client waits until months or years after the accident, and certain mistakes or problems develop, the attorney is stuck dealing with whatever has happened. I usually have a handful of cases every year where had the client hired me much sooner in the process it would have made the difference of obtaining tens of thousands of dollars more in settlement (and this is after deducting my fee!).

6. The client hides past accidents from the lawyer. Once you begin a case, the other side is allowed to explore your past accident history to determine whether your injury or condition could have been caused by another accident. Usually the other side already has substantial information about your prior accidents. The insurance industry regularly keeps an extensive data base about people who have been in prior accidents and asserted claims. If you hide a prior accident history, either from your lawyer or the insurance company, this can severely damage your case if not destroy it.

7. The client hides past injuries or medical conditions from the lawyer. This should be obvious. You need to inform your lawyer about injuries or medical conditions that pre-existed the accident. If you saw a doctor before the accident you can bet there is a written record (i.e., chart note) that describes it in detail. If your lawyer knows about your prior medical history in the beginning, than he or she can do something about it or at least manage the case in an appropriate way to minimize its damaging effect on your current case. But if you hide this information and your lawyer finds out later on you will either lose your case or cause your lawyer to fire you as a client.

8. The client makes damaging statements to the doctor and they show up in the records. You need to be aware that any statement you make to your doctor can show up in the medical records and then be a permanent "record" in the case. For example, describing your injury as "not that bad" or describing the accident as "minor" or the collision as a "bump" or "fender bender" can come back to haunt you if your injuries turn out to be worse than first thought or if your case ever gets in front of a jury.

9. The client fails to make medical appointments or has "gaps" in treatment. Clients who miss appointments or who stop and begin treatment after several weeks or months can seriously damage the case. Jurors don't believe someone is really that injured if that person misses a lot of medical appointments. It can also be extremely difficult to prove that treatment received after a significant "gap" in time following the accident was actually caused by that accident. When people stop treatment for a significant period of time, jurors tend to believe that the person recovered from their injuries.

10. The client misrepresents his or her activity level. Insurance companies routinely hire private investigators to monitor people who claim they were injured in an accident. With advances in technology (miniature cameras and video recorders) it can be extremely easy to record your public activities. If you misrepresent your limitations or activity level to your lawyer or your doctors and the insurance company can show jurors contradictory "hidden camera" footage, your credibility will be destroyed and so will your case. Don't do it.

Chapter Ten

"Top Ten Myths" Lists

Over the years I've compiled some lists of "Top Ten Myths" based on common misperceptions and erroneous beliefs concerning accident cases and the lawyers that handle them.

Top Ten Myths About Auto Accident Claims

There is a lot of erroneous information out there about accident claims. Here are my "Top Ten" myths:

Myth #1   You have to give a recorded
statement to the at-fault driver's
insurance company or your claim
will be denied.

Myth #2   You have to sign a medical
authorization at the request of the at
fault driver's insurance company so
it can go fishing into your past

	medical history, or your claim will be denied.
Myth #3	If you submit a reasonable settlement demand to the insurance company, you will get a reasonable settlement offer.
Myth #4	The amount of your settlement should be three times the amount of your medical bills (or four times, or five times, etc.).
Myth #5	The at-fault driver's insurance company is obligated to pay for your medical bills as they become due.
Myth #6	If you file a claim with your own auto insurance company, it will treat you better than the at-fault driver's insurance company.
Myth #7	If you get in an accident that was not your fault, there will be enough insurance to pay for all of your bills, lost wages and injuries.
Myth #8	You can expect to get the same settlement that your cousin (or neighbor, or friend, or co-worker, etc.) received for his or her accident

	claim with similar injuries.
Myth #9	The jury will give you money for all of your past medical bills because your doctor says you were injured.
Myth #10	The court system is like a lottery for injury claims that will help you get rich.

Top Ten Myths About Personal Injury Lawyers

There are many myths about personal injury lawyers. Here are what I consider to be the "Top Ten":

Myth #1:	All personal injury lawyers have basically the same training and experience.
Myth #2:	Any lawyer that graduates from law school can try a personal injury case in court.
Myth #3:	All personal injury lawyers go to trial at some point.
Myth #4:	A personal injury lawyer that never goes to trial can get just as good settlements as one that does go to trial.

Myth #5:	A lawyer who is good at "DUI" cases or "real estate law" will all so be good at personal injury cases.
Myth #6:	The personal injury lawyer who advertises on T.V. must be a great lawyer and super successful or else he couldn't afford the expensive commercial.
Myth #7:	The personal injury lawyer who takes out big glossy ads in the Yellow Pages is usually the best lawyer to choose.
Myth #8:	A "lawyer referral" service is always a good way to find the right lawyer for your case.
Myth #9:	The bar association determines whether a lawyer can advertise that he is a "personal injury specialist."
Myth #10:	The personal injury lawyer who advertises will actually be the lawyer who handles your case.

Chapter Eleven

Questions About Insurance

The Minimum Insurance Requirements for Washington State

Many states have laws that require motorists to purchase a minimum amount of automobile liability insurance. In Washington State, a motorist must purchase a liability policy with minimum coverage of at least $25,000 per person and $50,000 per occurrence. The amount of your liability coverage is the maximum amount of coverage to pay for damages that you cause another. A policy that has coverage of $25,000/$50,000 is the minimum amount necessary before you can legally operate a motor vehicle in Washington. The "per person" limit means that the most money any one person can recover from the carrier for damages caused by a single accident is $25,000. The "per occurrence" limit means that the most money the insurance company will pay out for any one accident (or "occurrence") is $50,000. So if you had a "minimum limits" policy and you cause an accident, the most your insurance company will pay to any one person is $25,000. If the accident injured several people, your company will pay no more than $50,000 total even if the combined value of the claims exceeds $50,000.

In Washington, an automobile insurance carrier must offer other specific types of coverage on your auto policy. One of these types of coverage is called Personal Injury Protection (PIP). PIP is considered no-fault coverage that pays for medical treatment, lost wages and charges for reasonable domestic services that were incurred as a result of an accident. The term "no-fault" means that PIP coverage is available to anyone injured in an accident, regardless of who was at fault for causing the accident. PIP coverage is designed to pay for your past medical charges and lost wages in a timely fashion, so people do not have to wait to settle their accident claim. You can reject PIP coverage, but your rejection must be recorded in writing. If you reject PIP coverage, but your rejection is not recorded in writing your insurance company may still be required to pay you PIP benefits.

Another type of coverage that must be offered by the insurance company is called Uninsured/Underinsured Motorist (UIM) coverage. The purpose of UIM coverage is to compensate you for damages caused by an uninsured motorist or by a motorist who does not have enough insurance to fully compensate you for your damages. Just like PIP coverage, the insurance company must offer you UIM coverage unless you reject this coverage in writing. Your UIM coverage will equal the amount of your liability coverage unless you specify in writing a different amount. Statistics show that most accidents are caused by people who are uninsured or who don't carry enough automobile liability insurance. Therefore, you should always purchase as much UIM coverage as you can afford.

When the other driver has no insurance or not enough insurance

Many times an accident is caused by someone who either has no insurance or not enough insurance to pay for all of the damages. If you find yourself in this situation, you may have a claim against your own insurance company for Uninsured or Underinsured Motorist (UIM) benefits. If you have UIM coverage, then your insurance company must pay for all of the damages caused by the at-fault driver up to the policy maximum. Many people make the mistake of assuming that a UIM claim is easier to settle or resolve because they are dealing with their own insurance company. This simply is not true. The law allows your insurance company to assert all defenses which were available to the at-fault driver. For example, if there's a question about whether the other driver was 100% at fault, then your own insurance company may try to argue that you or someone else was partially at fault and then reduce the amount of your claim accordingly. You need to know that if you pursue a UIM claim, it does not matter to your insurance company that you have been a loyal customer for twenty years or that you have never before had to make a claim. What matters to your carrier is paying out little as possible. Therefore, you may benefit from the services of a personal injury attorney even if you are pursuing a claim against your own insurance company.

Should I apply for benefits under my own insurance policy?

If you've been injured by another person and you have PIP or UIM coverage, it is usually worthwhile to file a claim with your own insurance company. In Washington there are special rules and regulations that apply to PIP and UIM claims. These rules and regulations can offer special protections to you. They can also give your insurance company special rights, like forcing you to attend an involuntary medical examination by a doctor of their own choosing. Sometimes insurance companies either ignore or intentionally violate these regulations in an effort to save the company money. So you may want to consult with an experienced personal injury lawyer if you have any questions, or if you are having problems with your own insurance company paying these types of benefits.

Does My Own Insurance Company Have to Be Reimbursed?

If your medical bills were paid by health insurance, or by PIP, then you need to be aware that the carrier may assert a claim for reimbursement out of your personal injury recovery. Why is this so? Because most policies now have what are called "subrogation" or "reimbursement" provisions that require you to pay back any benefits you receive. Your "insurance" really becomes just a "loan." This may not seem fair, but it's perfectly legal. I have handled cases where the client's own insurance company has attempted to take nearly the entire personal injury settlement as "reimbursement" for the benefits already paid! However, the law allows certain defenses and exceptions to this type of claim which may entitle you to pay back only a small portion or nothing at all. If you are faced with this situation from your own insurance company, you really do need to speak to an experienced personal injury attorney about your rights.

Chapter Twelve
What You and Juries Don't Know...

Most people are very surprised to learn about certain facts and procedures that occur in our legal system, and that are very common in personal injury claims. For example, did you know...

* If your case goes to trial, the jury will never know or be informed whether the defendant has insurance. The law in Washington is that the attorneys and judge are prohibited from even mentioning whether a party is insured. If one of the parties tells the jury that a defendant has insurance to pay the verdict, a mistrial will likely occur. This means the trial would have to start all over again.
* Practically speaking, if a lawsuit is filed in court or if the case goes to trial, the defendant will almost always have insurance to pay a verdict. A plaintiff's lawyer will not devote upwards of 100 to 200 hours or more to pursue a case unless there is a guaranteed

source of recovery (i.e., an insurance policy to pay a verdict). If you find yourself on a jury in a civil case, rest assured the defendant will have the means to pay any verdict that is handed down.

✳ Even though the jury will never be informed about the defendant's insurance company, the company still hires and pays the defendant's lawyer, decides when to settle, and pretty much makes all of the decisions involved in the case. Most of the time a defendant has little, if any, say about how the case is defended or if a settlement should occur. Decisions about whether to settle and how much to settle are always made by the defendant's insurance company.

✳ Filing a lawsuit does not automatically mean your case will be decided by a jury. In fact, many if not most personal injury attorneys would rather have a judge decide the case instead of a jury. This is because too many jurors are highly suspicious and skeptical of injured plaintiffs, and often refuse to give adequate compensation for legitimate injuries based on a variety of reasons. To have your case resolved by a jury, you must file a specific document with the court and pay a fee.

✳ Most of the time (90% or more) it is the defendant's insurance company that requests a jury and pays the required fee to the court! Why? Because the insurance industry knows that juries will typically award less money (and sometimes no money) in personal injury cases than compared with the amount a judge will award.

Chapter Thirteen

Why I Wrote This Book

I have been representing individuals in car accident cases since 1994. I have devoted my entire law practice to accident and injury claims. That's all I do. So if you want a lawyer to help you with a divorce or a business problem or some type of real estate transaction, then I can't help you. I've encountered too many situations where the person injured in an accident was taken advantage of by the insurance company or the person made some serious mistakes that damaged the claim. I wrote this book because I believe consumers who have been injured in an accident deserve to have good accurate information about the claims process and how to deal with the insurance company. I also believe that consumers should have enough information to help them find and hire a good personal injury lawyer for their accident case. The decision to hire an attorney is an important one. The lawyer you hire can make a big difference on the outcome of your case. In some cases, the lawyer you choose can have long lasting consequences – good or bad.

I also wrote this book because I am tired of the outrageous advertising claims made by some lawyers, many of whom have never even tried an accident case in court. I can't tell you the number of times I have been contacted by an accident victim who has already hired a lawyer only to find out that the lawyer is inexperienced or has bungled and damaged the case in some way. Unfortunately, I have to tell these people that there is little I can do for them after a serious mistake has been made. I wish they had hired me or someone else experienced in personal injury law from the very beginning.

Another reason I wrote this book is because I am disturbed by the number of lawyers who run large marketing campaigns (T.V. and Yellow Pages) for the sole purpose of creating "volume injury practices." These law firms can't possibly devote enough attention to any one case to achieve the best possible result for the client. Often times these lawyers see clients only as "dollar signs." They sign up as many clients as possible so they can settle them very quickly to earn their fee and then move on to the next case. Unfortunately for you (the consumer) this "volume" approach is often not in your best interest.

And finally, I wrote this book because, frankly, it saves me a lot of time speaking to prospective clients and accident victims who contact my office. There's a ton of information in this book that can answer many of the questions I receive each day from people who call me. I cannot, and will not, take on every case. Each month I turn down good cases that do not meet my case selection criteria. Therefore, this book can also help you decide whether your case meets my criteria. But if you should choose to handle your own claim then this book will help you navigate through the claims process when dealing with the insurance company. Even if I do not accept your case, I consider it my duty as a lawyer to educate consumers about the claims process so they do not fall prey to the insurance company, or make the wrong choice when hiring an inexperienced or unqualified attorney.

Most law firms or attorneys who specialize in car accident cases will offer you a "Free Consultation." Many times, particularly in the volume practices, at the initial consultation the attorney will engage in pressure tactics to convince you to sign on the dotted line. This book will arm you with the knowledge and information necessary for you to make a smart decision about hiring a lawyer before you are subject to the pressure tactics of a smooth talking lawyer. If you've been injured in an accident and you are looking for an attorney to help you, then you owe it to yourself to read this book.

This Book Is Not Intended to Give Legal Advice

I wouldn't be worth my salt as a lawyer if I didn't include the appropriate legal disclaimer. Therefore, I have to make it clear that this book is not intended to give legal advice. Nor is it intended to substitute for legal counsel about your case. I am prohibited from giving you legal advice about your case unless you hire me or my office and we agree in writing to accept your case and work on your behalf. I wrote this book for informational purposes only. That is, this book should be used by you to gather as much information as necessary to help you understand the claims process and to help you make smart decisions about your accident case. If you should wish to hire me or my office for your case, then you can read further in the book about our case selection criteria.

Chapter Fourteen
About My Practice

Several years ago and after handling hundreds of accident cases, I decided that I wanted to limit the number and types of cases that my office will accept. My office does not operate a "high volume" personal injury law firm. We don't advertise on T.V. or buy big yellow page ads like many of the "personal injury mill" law firms you may be familiar with. We don't need to handle hundreds of cases each year to be successful. We don't handle every type of injury case under the sun, like slip and falls, discrimination or defective products. We don't have to, and quite frankly, we don't want to.

I am highly selective about the cases my office will take on. Unlike the "personal injury mills," I don't allow paralegals and assistants to negotiate a case with the insurance company. Fewer cases means more attention and better results for my clients, not to mention a more satisfying lifestyle for me and my staff.

I know of many personal injury attorneys who have never even tried an accident case in court. Many of them never even meet the client, let alone perform substantial legal work on the client's behalf. If you hire a lawyer, don't you think you should at least meet that lawyer before trusting him or her with a case that may have long-lasting consequences for you? Yet this is common place with many of the attorneys who work at the large "personal injury mill" law firms. That's not what I want, for me or my clients.

I have been handling accident cases in the state of Washington since 1994. My practice is devoted 100% to personal injury law and accident cases. That's all I do. I don't handle any other type of case. Most of my clients are referred to me by satisfied clients and other attorneys. Sometimes I get referrals from defense attorneys and mediators whom I faced or met in prior litigation. If my office accepts your case, and you don't live nearby our office, we will often come to you.

Sometimes the best advice I can give a client is that the case cannot be won, or that the risk and cost of pursuing the case is simply too great for the client to incur. Other times I'll tell the client that he or she is best served by handling the case on their own because it is too small for my office to take on. Still other times I am willing to guarantee that the client will receive more money in settlement than the insurance company's "last offer."

If my office accepts your case, you can be assured that you will receive personal attention from my staff and me, and together we will vigorously pursue the case against the insurance company and their lawyers until the best possible result is obtained. I understand that if a lawsuit is filed, it could be the most important event of your life at that time. I then will personally handle your lawsuit. Your case will be handled by an attorney, not a paralegal or a "case manager."

My office has represented hundreds of people harmed by the negligence of others over the years, including those injured by the negligent acts of corporations, the state of Washington, cities and other governmental entities. We routinely handle auto accident claims, medical malpractice, construction accidents, wrongful death and insurance claims.

You can learn more about my office and me at our website: www.InjuryTrialLawyer.com. This is the most popular small firm website in the Pacific Northwest. We regularly update the site with new information and informative articles about many topics.

Chapter Fifteen

The Cases Do I Not Accept

Due to the high volume of calls we receive from accident victims and referrals from other attorneys, I have found that the only way to provide high quality service and personal attention to my clients is to limit the type of accident cases that my office will accept. I have imposed strict criteria for this purpose. Although I would love to help everyone who has been in an accident, I'm sure you can understand that this would be impossible, if not impractical, particularly when my practice is focused on high quality and individual attention that many of the other "high volume" personal injury practices cannot offer. For these reasons, my office will generally not accept the following types of cases:

* Accidents involving minor impact or little or no visible damage to the vehicle. My experience with juries is that they do not believe a minor impact can cause serious injury. I have tried many cases where the doctors testified that my client was injured, but the photographs and repair estimates showed little or

no damage to the vehicle. Sometimes the verdict in these types of cases was very low and therefore did not justify the expense and effort of taking the case to trial. Although I have won these types of cases and achieved very high verdicts as well, the risk to the client of a very low verdict is just too great. Therefore, I will often decline a case if the property damage amounts to no more than a few hundred dollars. There are exceptions, of course.

* Cases with less than $10,000 in expected medical bills. In most instances, your case must have at least $10,000 in past and future medical bills before my office will agree to represent you.[5] If your medical bills are currently less than $10,000 but you expect that this amount will increase to more than $10,000 over time, than my office can help you. We certainly would like to take on every case that needs a good attorney, but we cannot. For this reason, I have decided that cases where the expected medical bills are less than $10,000, are just too small for us to effectively handle. There are other attorneys who are willing to accept this type of case and we can provide you with a list of names.

* Cases where you were found to be at fault by the police. I will not represent you if you were charged or cited by the police for causing the accident. Even if you disagree, or even if you say the police officer

was wrong, I still will not represent you. I understand that police officers make mistakes, but if after interviewing the witnesses and inspecting the scene the police officer decides that you were at fault and not the other driver, I will not represent you.

＊ Cases where you were found to be mostly at fault by the police. Even if the other driver shares some blame, if the police determined that you were mostly at fault, then I will not represent you. But if the other driver was mostly at fault, I may be willing to help depending on the other facts involved in your case.

＊ Cases where you have had a serious or long-standing pre-existing injury or condition to the same body part injured in the accident. If you injured your back in the accident, but you have had a chronic ongoing back problem for the last 10 years then usually I will not represent you. If you injured your neck in the accident, but you had three (3) prior surgeries on your neck or treated with a chiropractor for 10 years before the accident, then I will probably not represent you. Juries will not usually award a substantial amount of money for injuries where the person injured had a longstanding problem to the same body part. Again, I feel it is not worth the risk of taking these types of cases to trial.

＊ Cases where you have had several other accidents or claims before this one. I can't accept your case if you have had several prior accidents or injury claims. These cases are almost always difficult to settle with the insurance company and a lawsuit is pretty much inevitable. Furthermore, juries are not kind to people who have a significant accident history.

* Cases where the statute of limitations will expire soon. I like to have at least thirty (30) days, and sometimes more time than this, to adequately investigate and prepare your case. If you come to me within a few weeks or days before the statute of limitations will expire, I will usually decline your case. You have to understand that a case that only has a few weeks or days before the statute expires will require immediate attention, even if it interferes with my other cases and the precious time I have with my family. I have decided that another person's procrastination will not become my crisis if I can help it.

* Cases where you have a significant and prior criminal record involving fraud, deceit or dishonesty. Clients who have a criminal history, particularly one that involves fraud, deceit or dishonesty, can cause enormous problems at trial. Since credibility of the injured person is often extremely important in personal injury cases, I will not agree to represent someone with a prior criminal history involving fraud, deceit or dishonesty.

As I have said before, my office represents many people with valid claims. But I have found that if I do not adopt strict criteria for the selection of cases, my other clients can suffer the consequences with decreased personal attention and lesser quality of service. I don't want to spend most of time on many little cases that may each have a "problem" or "challenge." If I do, this can cause my other legitimate cases to suffer. That's why I've made the decision to keep my case load small, and concentrate my efforts on increasing the value of those good cases that meet my selection criteria.

About the Author

Washington attorney Christopher Michael Davis has been representing individuals in accident cases and against insurance companies since 1994. In 2006, he was named a Rising Star Attorney by Washington Law & Politics magazine (this recognition is given only to the top 2.5% of lawyers age 40 and under in Washington State). In 2007, Washington Law & Politics named Mr. Davis a Super Lawyer (the top 5% of lawyers in Washington). Mr. Davis speaks at Continuing Legal Education seminars on topics related to personal injury. He teaches and instructs other lawyers in Washington State on topics such as jury selection, proving damages and developing winning trial techniques. Mr. Davis has been licensed to practice law in Washington State since 1993. He has obtained millions of dollars in verdicts and settlements for his clients. Mr. Davis is a member of numerous professional organizations, including the Washington State Trial Lawyers Association,

American Association for Justice, and the North American Brain Injury Society. For a sampling of verdicts and settlements achieved by Mr. Davis in a variety of cases, please visit www.InjuryTrialLawyer.com.

Footnotes

[1] See Jones vs. Allstate Insurance Co., 146Wn.2d291 (2002).

[2] See the IRC's website at www.ircweb.org.

[3] In this author's experience, and all things being equal, juries typically award more damages to people they like and trust. If the client makes a good impression then this will increase the likelihood of obtaining a favorable verdict or settlement.

[4] There are exceptions of course, depending on the facts of the case. That is why you should always consult with an experienced attorney if you have a question about what time limit may apply to your case.

[5] If you live in the state of Washington call us for a referral for another type of attorney. I have relationships with good attorneys in many different specialties. My office does not charge for this service.

WA